W9-BIA-023

Rookie reader®

The Long Way Home

By Larry Dane Brimner
Illustrated by Terry Sirrell

Children's Press®
A Division of Grolier Publishing
New York • London • Hong Kong • Sydney
Danbury, Connecticut

For Mark Friedman
—L. D. B.

For my wonderful wife Eileen, our miracle daughter Flynn,
and my mother, who helps out with everything.
—T. S.

Reading Consultants
Linda Cornwell
Coordinator of School Quality and Professional Improvement
(Indiana State Teachers Association)

Katharine A. Kane
Education Consultant
(Retired, San Diego County Office of Education
and San Diego State University)

Visit Children's Press® on the Internet at:
http://publishing.grolier.com

Library of Congress Cataloging-in-Publication Data
Brimner, Larry Dane.
    The long way home / by Larry Dane Brimner ; illustrated by Terry Sirrell.
      p. cm. — (Rookie reader)
    Summary: A child takes the long way home in order to collect an array of new pets.
    ISBN 0-516-22011-X (lib. bdg.)   0-516-27078-8 (pbk.)
    [1. Animals—Fiction. 2. Pets—Fiction.   3. Stories in rhyme.] I. Sirrell, Terry, ill. II.
Title. III. Series.
PZ8.3.B77145 Lo 2000
[E]—dc21   99-057168

I took the long way home today.

Guess what followed me all the way.

One brown dog.

One plump cat.

9

One pink hog.

11

One round rat.

13

It was hard work,
I have to say.

But step by step

16

they came my way.

Well . . . treat by treat, they followed. Hooray!

19

They followed me from there to here.

22

They followed me.
I hope that's clear.

Aren't they sweet?
They want to cuddle.

They'll be neat.
I'll clean that puddle.

Mom, they need a place to stay . . .
and a kid to call their own.

29

Oh, *please*, don't say, "No way."

Word List (68 words)

a	from	neat	that
all	guess	need	that's
and	hard	no	the
aren't	have	oh	their
be	here	one	there
brown	hog	own	they
but	home	pink	they'll
by	hooray	place	to
call	hope	please	today
came	I	plump	took
cat	I'll	puddle	treat
clean	it	rat	want
clear	kid	round	was
cuddle	long	say	way
dog	me	stay	well
don't	Mom	step	what
followed	my	sweet	work

About the Author

Larry Dane Brimner is the author of many Rookie Readers, including *How Many Ants?*, *Dinosaurs Dance*, and *Nana's Hog*. He lives in San Diego, California.

About the Illustrator

Terry Sirrell has been a cartoonist and illustrator for the past sixteen years. His cartoons and characters have appeared on the backs of cereal boxes, in the advertising of numerous major corporations, and in dozens of publications. Terry also illustrates children's books, greeting cards, and jigsaw puzzles.